The early history of the airplane

Orville Wright, Wilbur Wright

Nabu Public Domain Reprints:

You are holding a reproduction of an original work published before 1923 that is in the public domain in the United States of America, and possibly other countries. You may freely copy and distribute this work as no entity (individual or corporate) has a copyright on the body of the work. This book may contain prior copyright references, and library stamps (as most of these works were scanned from library copies). These have been scanned and retained as part of the historical artifact.

This book may have occasional imperfections such as missing or blurred pages, poor pictures, errant marks, etc. that were either part of the original artifact, or were introduced by the scanning process. We believe this work is culturally important, and despite the imperfections, have elected to bring it back into print as part of our continuing commitment to the preservation of printed works worldwide. We appreciate your understanding of the imperfections in the preservation process, and hope you enjoy this valuable book.

LIBRARY
UNIVERSITY OF CALIFORNIA
DAVIS

The Wright Brothers' Aeroplane

By Orville and Wilbur Wright

THOUGH the subject of aerial navigation is generally considered new, it has occupied the minds of men more or less from the earliest ages. Our personal interest in it dates from our childhood days. Late in the autumn of 1878 our father came into the house one evening with some object partly concealed in his hands, and before we could see what it was, he tossed it into the air. Instead of falling to the floor, as we expected, it flew across the room, till it struck the ceiling, where it fluttered awhile, and finally sank to the floor. It was a little toy, known to scientists as a "helicoptere," but which we, with sublime disregard for science, at once dubbed a "bat." It was a light frame of cork and bamboo, covered with paper, which formed two screws, driven in opposite directions by rubber bands under torsion. A toy so delicate lasted only a short time in the hands of small boys, but its memory was abiding.

Several years later we began building these helicopteres for ourselves, making each one larger than that preceding. But, to our astonishment, we found that the larger the "bat" the less it flew. We did not know that a machine having only twice the linear dimensions of another would require eight times the power. We finally became discouraged, and returned to kite-flying, a sport to which we had devoted so much attention that we were regarded as experts. But as we became older we had to give up this fascinating sport as unbecoming to boys of our ages.

It was not till the news of the sad death of Lilienthal reached America in the summer of 1896 that we again gave more than passing attention to the subject of flying. We then studied with great interest Chanute's "Progress in Flying Machines," Langley's "Experiments in Aerodynamics," the "Aeronautical Annuals" of 1905, 1906, and 1907, and several pamphlets published by the Smithsonian Institution, especially articles by Lilienthal and extracts from Mouillard's "Empire of the Air." The larger works gave us a good understanding of the nature of the flying problem, and the difficulties in past attempts to solve it, while Mouillard and Lilienthal, the great missionaries of the flying cause, infected us with their own unquenchable enthusiasm, and transformed idle curiosity into the active zeal of workers.

In the field of aviation there were two schools. The first, represented by such men as Professor Langley and Sir Hiram Maxim, gave chief attention to power flight; the second, represented by Lilienthal, Mouillard, and Chanute, to soaring flight. Our sympathies were with the latter school, partly from impatience at the wasteful extravagance of mounting delicate and costly machinery on wings which no one knew how to manage, and partly, no doubt, from the extraordinary charm and enthusiasm with which the apostles of soaring flight set forth the beauties of sailing through the air on fixed wings, deriving the motive power from the wind itself.

The balancing of a flyer may seem, at first thought, to be a very simple matter, yet almost every experimenter had found in this one point which he could not satisfactorily master. Many different methods were tried. Some experimenters placed the center of gravity far below the wings, in the belief that the weight would naturally seek to remain at the lowest point. It is true, that, like the pendulum, it tended to seek the lowest point; but also, like the pendulum, it tended to oscillate in a manner destructive of all stability. A more satisfactory system, especially for lateral balance, was that of arranging the wings in the shape of a broad V, to form a dihedral angle, with the center low and the wingtips elevated. In theory this was an automatic system, but in practice it had two serious defects: first, it tended to keep the machine oscillating; and second, its usefulness was restricted to calm air.

In a slightly modified form the same system was applied to the fore-and-aft balance. The main aeroplane was set at a positive angle, and a horizontal tail at a negative angle, while the center of gravity was placed far forward. As in the case of lateral control, there was a tendency to constant undulation, and the very forces which caused a restoration of balance in calms caused a disturbance of the balance in winds. Notwithstanding the known limitations of this principle, it had been embodied in almost every prominent flying machine which had been built.

After considering the practical effect of the dihedral principle, we reached the conclusion that a flyer founded upon it might be of interest from a scientific point of view, but could be of no value in a practical way. We therefore resolved to try a fundamentally different principle. We would arrange the machine so that it would not tend to right itself. We would make it as inert as possible to the effects of change of direction or speed, and thus reduce the effects of wind-gusts to a minimum. We would do this in the fore-and-aft stability by giving the aeroplanes a peculiar shape; and in the lateral balance by arching the surfaces from tip to tip, just the reverse of what our predecessors had done. Then by some suitable contrivance, actuated by the operator, forces should be brought into play to regulate the balance.

Lilienthal and Chanute had guided and balanced their machines, by shifting the weight of the operator's body. But this method seemed to us incapable of expansion to meet large conditions, because the weight to be moved and the distance of possible motion were limited, while the disturbing forces steadily increased, both with wing area and with wind velocity. In order to meet the needs of large machines, we wished to employ some system whereby the operator could vary at will the inclination of different parts of the wings, and thus obtain from the wind forces to restore the balance which the wind itself had disturbed. This could easily be done by using wings capable of being warped, and by supplementary adjustable surfaces in the shape of rudders. As the forces obtainable for control would necessarily increase in the same ratio as the disturbing forces, the method seemed capable of expansion to an almost unlimited extent. A happy device was discovered whereby the apparently rigid system of superposed surfaces, invented by Wenham, and improved by Stringfellow and Chanute, could be warped in a most unexpected way, so that the aeroplanes could be presented on the right and left sides at different angles to the wind. This, with an adjustable, horizontal front rudder, formed the main feature of our first glider.

The period from 1885 to 1900 was one of unexampled activity in aeronautics, and for a time there was high hope that the age of flying was at hand. But Maxim, after spending $100,000, abandoned the work; the Ader machine, built at the expense of the French Government, was a failure; Lilienthal and Pilcher were killed in experiments; and Chanute and many others, from one cause or another, had relaxed their efforts, though it subsequently became known that Professor Langley was still secretly at work on a machine for the United States Government. The public, discouraged by the failures and tragedies just witnessed, considered flight beyond the reach of man, and classed its adherents with the inventors of perpetual motion.

We began our active experiments at the close of this period, in October, 1900, at Kitty Hawk, North Carolina. Our machine was designed to be flown as a kite, with a man on board, in winds from 15 to 20 miles an hour. But, upon trial, it was found that much stronger winds were required to lift it. Suitable winds not being plentiful, we found it necessary, in order to test the new balancing system, to fly the machine as a kite without a man on board, operating the levers through cords from the ground. This did not give the practice anticipated, but it inspired confidence in the new system of balance.

In the summer of 1901 we became personally acquainted with Mr. Chanute. When he learned that we were interested in flying as a sport, and not with any expectation of recovering the money we were expending on it, he gave us much encouragement. At our invitation, he spent several weeks with us at our camp at Kill Devil Hill, four miles south of Kitty Hawk, during our experiments of that and the two succeeding years. He also witnessed one flight of the power machine near Dayton, Ohio, in October, 1904.

The machine of 1901 was built with the shape of surface used by Lilienthal, curved from front to rear like the segment of a parabola, with a curvature 1/12 the depth of its cord; but to make doubly sure that it would have sufficient lifting capacity when flown as a kite in 15 or 20-mile winds, we increased the area from 165 square feet, used in 1900, to 308 square feet—a size much larger than Lilienthal, Pilcher, or Chanute had deemed safe. Upon trial, however, the lifting capacity again fell very far short of calculation, so that the idea of securing practice while flying as a kite had to be abandoned. Mr. Chanute, who witnessed the experiments, told us that the trouble was not due to poor construction of the machine. We saw only one other explanation—that the tables of air-pressures in general use were incorrect.

We then turned to gliding—coasting downhill on the air—as the only method of getting the desired practice in balancing a machine. After a few minutes' practice we were able to make glides of over 300 feet, and in a few days were safely operating in 27-mile winds. In these experiments we met with several unexpected phenomena. We found that, contrary to the teachings of the books, the center of pressure on a curved surface traveled backward when the surface was inclined, at small angles, more and more edgewise to the wind. We also discovered that in free flight, when the wing on one side of the machine was presented to the wind at a greater angle than the one on the other side, the wing with the greater angle descended, and the machine turned in a direction just the reverse of

3

what we were led to expect when flying the machine as a kite. The larger angle gave more resistance to forward motion, and reduced the speed of the wing on that side. The decrease in speed more than counterbalanced the effect of the larger angle. The addition of a fixed vertical vane in the rear increased the trouble, and made the machine absolutely dangerous. It was some time before a remedy was discovered. This consisted of movable rudders working in conjunction with the twisting of the wings. The details of this arrangement are given in specifications published several years ago.

The experiments of 1901 were far from encouraging. Although Mr. Chanute assured us that, both in control and in weight carried per horse-power, the results obtained were better than those of any of our predecessors, yet we saw that the calculations upon which all flying machines had been based were unreliable, and that all were simply groping in the dark. Having set out with absolute faith in the existing scientific data, we were driven to doubt one thing after another, till finally, after two years of experiment, we cast it all aside, and decided to rely entirely upon our own investigations. Truth and error were everywhere so intimately mixed as to be undistinguishable. Nevertheless, the time expended in preliminary study of books was not misspent, for they gave us a good general understanding of the subject, and enabled us at the outset to avoid effort in many directions in which results would have been hopeless.

The standard measurements of windpressures is the force produced by a current of air of one mile per hour velocity striking square against a plane of one square foot area. The practical difficulties of obtaining an exact measurement of this force have been great. The measurements by different recognized authorities vary 50 per cent. When this simplest of measurements presents so great difficulties, what shall be said of the troubles encountered by those who attempt to find the pressure at each angle as the plane is inclined more and more edgewise to the wind? In the eighteenth century the French Academy prepared tables giving such information, and at a later date the Aeronautical Society of Great Britain made similar experiments. Many persons likewise published measurements and formulas; but the results were so discordant that Professor Langley undertook a new series of measurements, the results of which form the basis of his celebrated work, "Experiments in Aerodynamics." Yet a critical examination of the data upon which he based his conclusions as to the pressures at small angles shows results so various as to make many of his conclusions little better than guesswork.

To work intelligently, one needs to know the effects of a multitude of variations that could be incorporated in the surfaces of flying machines. The pressures on squares are different from those on rectangles, circles, triangles, or ellipses; arched surfaces differ from planes, and vary among themselves according to the depth of curvature; true arcs differ from parabolas, and the latter differ among themselves; thick surfaces differ from thin, and surfaces thicker in one place than another vary in pressure when the positions of maximum thickness are different; some surfaces are most efficient at one angle, others at other angles. The shape of the edge also makes a difference, so that thousands of combinations are possible in so simple a thing as a wing.

We had taken up aeronautics merely as a sport. We reluctantly entered upon the scientific side of it. But we soon found the work so fascinating that we were drawn into it deeper and deeper. Two testing machines were built, which we believed would avoid the errors to which the measurements of others had been subject. After making preliminary measurements on a great number of different-shaped surfaces, to secure a general understanding of the subject, we began systematic measurements of standard surfaces, so varied in design as to bring out the underlying causes of differences noted in their pressures. Measurements were tabulated on nearly 50 of these at all angles from zero to 45 degrees at intervals of 2½ degrees. Measurements were also secured showing the effects on each other when surfaces are superposed, or when they follow one another.

Some strange results were obtained. One surface, with a heavy roll at the front edge, showed the same lift for all angles from 7½ to 45 degrees. A square plane, contrary to the measurements of all our predecessors, gave a greater pressure at 30 degrees than at 45 degrees. This seemed so anomalous that we were almost ready to doubt our own measurements, when a simple test was suggested. A weather-vane, with two planes attached to the pointer at an angle of 80 degrees with each other, was made. According to our tables, such a vane would be in unstable equilibrium when pointing directly into the wind; for if by chance the wind should happen to strike one plane at 39 degrees and the other at 41 degrees, the plane with the smaller angle would have the greater pressure, and the pointer would be turned still farther out of the course of the wind until the two vanes again secured equal pressures, which would be at approximately 30 and 50 degrees. But the vane performed in this very manner. Further corroboration of the tables was obtained in experiments with the new glider at Kill Devil Hill the next season.

In September and October, 1902, nearly 1,000 gliding flights were made, several of which covered distances of over 600 feet. Some, made against a wind of 36 miles an hour, gave proof of the effectiveness of the devices for control. With this machine, in the autumn of 1903, we made a number of flights in which we remained in the air for over a minute, often soaring for a considerable time in one spot, without any descent at all. Little wonder that our unscientific assistant should think the only thing needed to keep it indefinitely in the air would be a coat of feathers to make it light!

With accurate data for making calculations, and a system of balance effective in winds as well as in calms, we were now in a position, we thought, to build a successful power-flyer. The first designs provided for a total weight of 600 lbs., including the operator and an eight horse-power motor. But, upon completion, the motor gave more power than had been estimated, and this allowed 150 lbs. to be added for strengthening the wings and other parts.

Our tables made the designing of the wings an easy matter, and as screw-propellers are simply wings traveling in a spiral course, we anticipated no trouble from this source. We had thought of getting the theory of the screw-propeller from the marine engineers, and then, by applying our tables of air-pressures to their formulas, of designing air-propellers suitable for our purpose. But so far as we could learn, the marine engineers possessed only empirical formulas, and the exact action of the screw-propeller, after a century of use, was still very obscure. As we were not in a position to undertake a long series of practical experiments to discover a propeller suitable for our machine, it seemed necessary to obtain such a thorough understanding of the theory of its reactions as would enable us to design them from calculations alone. What at first seemed a problem became more complex the longer we studied it. With the machine moving forward, the air flying backward, the propellers turning sidewise, and nothing standing still, it seemed impossible to find a starting-point from which to trace the various simultaneous reactions. Contemplation of it was confusing. After long arguments we often found ourselves in the ludicrous position of each having been converted to the other's side, with no more agreement than when the discussion began.

It was not till several months had passed, and every phase of the problem had been thrashed over and over, that the various reactions began to untangle themselves. When once a clear understanding had been obtained there was no difficulty in designing suitable propellers, with proper diameter, pitch, and area of blade, to meet the requirements of the flyer. High efficiency in a screw-propeller is not dependent upon any particular or peculiar shape; and there is no such thing as a "best" screw. A propeller giving a high dynamic efficiency when used upon one machine may be almost worthless when used upon another. The propeller should in every case be designed to meet the particular conditions of the machine to which it is to be applied. Our first propellers, built entirely from calculation, gave in useful work 66 per cent. of the power expended. This was about one-third more than had been secured by Maxim or Langley.

The first flights with the power machine were made on December 17, 1903. Only five persons besides ourselves were present. These were Messrs. John T. Daniels, W. S. Dough, and A. D. Etheridge, of the Kill Devil Life-Saving Station; Mr. W. C. Brinkley, of Manteo; and Mr. John Ward, of Naghead. Although a general invitation had been extended to the people living within five or six miles, not many were willing to face the rigors of a cold December wind in order to see, as they no doubt thought, another flying machine not fly. The first flight lasted only 12 seconds, a flight very modest compared with that of birds, but it was, nevertheless, the first in the history of the world in which a machine carrying a man had raised itself by its own power into the air in free flight, had sailed forward on a level course without reduction of speed, and had finally landed without being wrecked. The second and third flights were a little longer, and the fourth lasted 59 seconds, covering a distance of 852 feet over the ground against a 20-mile wind.

After the last flight the machine was carried back to camp and set down in what was thought to be a safe place. But a few minutes later, while we were engaged in conversation about the flights, a sudden gust of wind struck the machine, and started to turn it over. All made a rush to stop it, but we were too late. Mr. Daniels, a giant in stature and strength, was lifted off his feet, and falling inside, between the surfaces, was

shaken about like a rattle in a box as the machine rolled over and over. He finally fell out upon the sand with nothing worse than painful bruises, but the damage to the machine caused a discontinuance of experiments.

In the spring of 1904, through the kindness of Mr. Torrence Huffman, of Dayton, Ohio, we were permitted to erect a shed, and to continue experiments, on what is known as the Huffman Prairie, at Simms Station, eight miles east of Dayton. The new machine was heavier and stronger, but similar to the one flown at Kill Devil Hill. When it was ready for its first trial every newspaper in Dayton was notified, and about a dozen representatives of the Press were present. Our only request was that no pictures be taken, and that the reports be unsensational, so as not to attract crowds to our experiment grounds. There were probably 50 persons altogether on the ground. When preparations had been completed a wind of only three or four miles was blowing—insufficient for starting on so short a track—but since many had come a long way to see the machine in action, an attempt was made. To add to the other difficulty, the engine refused to work properly. The machine, after running the length of the track, slid off the end without rising into the air at all. Several of the newspaper men returned the next day, but were again disappointed. The engine performed badly, and after a glide of only 60 feet, the machine came to the ground. Further trial was postponed till the motor could be put in better running condition. The reporters had now, no doubt, lost confidence in the machine, though their reports, in kindness, concealed it. Later, when they heard that we were making flights of several minutes' duration, knowing that longer flights had been made with airships, and not knowing any essential difference between airships and flying machines, they were but little interested.

We had not been flying long in 1904 before we found that the problem of equilibrium had not as yet been entirely solved. Sometimes, in making a circle, the machine would turn over sidewise despite anything the operator could do, although, under the same conditions in ordinary straight flight, it could have been righted in an instant. In one flight, in 1905, while circling around a honey locust tree at a height of about 50 feet, the machine suddenly began to turn up on one wing, and took a course toward the tree. The operator, not relishing the idea of landing in a thorn-tree, attempted to reach the ground. The left wing, however, struck the tree at a height of 10 or 12 feet from the ground and carried away several branches; but the flight, which had already covered a distance of six miles, was continued to the starting-point.

The causes of these troubles—too technical for explanation here—were not entirely overcome till the end of September, 1905. The flights then rapidly increased in length, till experiments were discontinued after October 5, on account of the number of people attracted to the field. Although made on a ground open on every side, and bordered on two sides by much-traveled thoroughfares, with electric cars passing every hour, and seen by all the people living in the neighborhood for miles around, and by several hundred others, yet these flights have been made by some newspapers the subject of a great "mystery."

A practical flyer having been finally realized, we spent the years 1906 and 1907 in constructing new machines and in business negotiations. It was not till May of this year that experiments (discontinued in October, 1905) were resumed at Kill Devil Hill, North Carolina. The recent flights were made to test the ability of our machine to meet the requirements of a contract with the United States Government to furnish a flyer capable of carrying two men and sufficient fuel supplies for a flight of 125 miles, with a speed of 40 miles an hour. The machine used in these tests was the same one with which the flights were made at Simms Station in 1905, though several changes had been made to meet present requirements. The operator assumed a sitting position, instead of lying prone, as in 1905, and a seat was added for a passenger. A larger motor was installed, and radiators and gasoline reservoirs of larger capacity replaced those previously used. No attempt was made to make high or long flights.

In order to show the general reader the way in which the machine operates, let us fancy ourselves ready for the start. The machine is placed upon a single-rail track facing the wind, and is securely fastened with a cable. The engine is put in motion, and the propellers in the rear whir. You take your seat at the center of the machine beside the operator. He slips the cable, and you shoot forward. An assistant who has been holding the machine in balance on the rail starts forward with you, but before you have gone 50 feet the speed is too great for him, and he lets go. Before reaching the end of the track the operator moves the front rudder, and the machine lifts from the rail like a kite supported by the pressure of the air underneath it. The ground under you is at first a perfect blur, but as you rise the objects become clearer. At a height of 100 feet you feel hardly any motion at all, except for the wind which strikes your face. If you did not take the precaution to fasten your hat before starting, you have probably lost it by this time. The operator moves a lever: the right wing rises, and the machine swings about to the left. You make a very short turn, yet you do not feel the sensation of being thrown from your seat, so often experienced in automobile and railway travel. You find yourself facing toward the point from which you started. The objects on the ground now seem to be moving at much higher speed, though you perceive no change in the pressure of the wind on your face. You know then that you are traveling with the wind. When you near the starting-point the operator stops the motor while still high in the air. The machine coasts down at an oblique angle to the ground, and after sliding 50 or 100 feet, comes to rest. Although the machine often lands when traveling at a speed of a mile a minute, you feel no shock whatever, and cannot, in fact, tell the exact moment at which it first touched the ground. The motor close beside you kept up an almost deafening roar during the whole flight, yet in your excitement you did not notice it till it stopped!

Our experiments have been conducted entirely at our own expense. In the beginning we had no thought of recovering what we were expending, which was not great, and was limited to what we could afford in recreation. Later, when a successful flight had been made with a motor, we gave up the business in which we were engaged, to devote our entire time and capital to the development of a machine for practical uses. As soon as our condition is such that constant attention to business is not required, we expect to prepare for publication the results of our laboratory experiments, which alone made an early solution of the flying problem possible.

How We Made the First Flight

By Orville Wright

THE flights of the 1902 glider had demonstrated the efficiency of our system of maintaining equilibrium, and also the accuracy of the laboratory work upon which the design of the glider was based. We then felt that we were prepared to calculate in advance the performance of machines with a degree of accuracy that had never been possible with the data and tables possessed by our predecessors. Before leaving camp in 1902 we were already at work on the general design of a new machine which we proposed to propel with a motor.

Immediately upon our return to Dayton, we wrote to a number of automobile and motor builders, stating the purpose for which we desired a motor, and asking whether they could furnish one that would develop eight brake-horsepower, with a weight complete not exceeding 200 pounds. Most of the companies answered that they were too busy with their regular business to undertake the building of such a motor for us; but one company replied that they had motors rated at 8 horse-power, according to the French system of ratings, which weighed only 135 pounds, and that if we thought this motor would develop enough power for our purpose they would be glad to sell us one. After an examination of the particulars of this motor, from which we learned that it had but a single cylinder of 4-inch bore and 5-inch stroke, we were afraid it was much over-rated. Unless the motor would develop a full 8 brake-horsepower, it would be useless for our purpose.

Finally we decided to undertake the building of the motor ourselves. We estimated that we could make one of four cylinders with 4-inch bore and 4-inch stroke, weighing not over two hundred pounds, including all accessories. Our only experience up to that time in the building of gasoline motors had been in the construction of an air-cooled motor, 5-inch bore and 7-inch stroke, which was used to run the machinery of our small workshop. To be certain that four cylinders of the size we had adopted (4" x 4") would develop the necessary 8 horsepower, we first fitted them in a temporary frame of simple and cheap construction. In just six weeks from the time the design was started, we had the motor on the block testing its power. The ability to do this so quickly was largely due to the enthusiastic and efficient services of Mr. C. E. Taylor, who did all the machine work in our shop for the first as well as the succeeding experimental machines. There was no provision for lubricating either cylinders or bearings while this motor was running. For that reason it was not possible to run it more than a minute or two at a time. In these short tests the motor developed about nine horse-power. We were then satisfied that, with proper lubrication and better adjustments, a little more power could

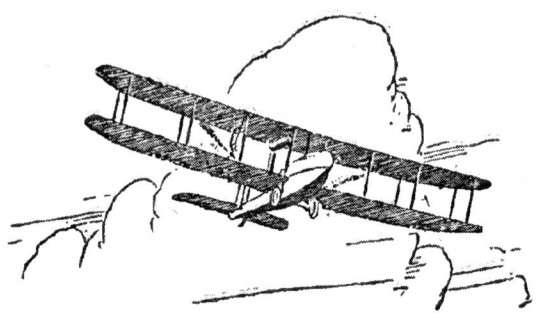

be expected. The completion of the motor according to drawing was, therefore, proceeded with at once.

While Mr. Taylor was engaged with this work, Wilbur and I were busy in completing the design of the machine itself. The preliminary tests of the motor having convinced us that more than 8 horse-power would be secured, we felt free to add enough weight to build a more substantial machine than we had originally contemplated.

* * * * * *

For two reasons we decided to use two propellers. In the first place we could, by the use of two propellers, secure a reaction against a greater quantity of air, and at the same time use a larger pitch angle than was possible with one propeller; and in the second place by having the propellers turn in opposite direction, the gyroscopic action of one would neutralize that of the other. The method we adopted of driving the propellers in opposite directions by means of chains is now too well known to need description here. We decided to place the motor to one side of the man, so that in case of a plunge headfirst, the motor could not fall upon him. In our gliding experiments we had had a number of experiences in which we had landed upon one wing, but the crushing of the wing had absorbed the shock, so that we were not uneasy about the motor in case of a landing of that kind. To provide against the machine rolling over forward in landing, we designed skids like sled runners, extending out in front of the main surfaces. Otherwise the general construction and operation of the machine was to be similar to that of the 1902 glider.

When the motor was completed and tested, we found that it would develop 16 horse-power for a few seconds, but that the power rapidly dropped till, at the end of a minute, it was only 12 horse-power. Ignorant of what a motor of this size ought to develop, we were greatly pleased with its performance. More experience showed us that we did not get one-half of the power we should have had.

With 12 horse-power at our command, we considered that we could permit the weight of the machine with operator to rise to 750 or 800 pounds, and still have as much surplus power as we had originally allowed for in the first estimate of 550 pounds.

Before leaving for our camp at Kitty Hawk we tested the chain drive for the propellers in our shop at Dayton, and found it satisfactory. We found, however, that our first propeller shafts, which were constructed of heavy gauge steel tubing, were not strong enough to stand the shocks received from a gasoline motor with light fly wheel, although they would have been able to transmit three or four times the power uniformly applied. We therefore built a new set of shafts of heavier tubing, which we tested and thought to be abundantly strong.

We left Dayton, September 23, and arrived at our camp at Kill Devil Hill on Friday, the 25th. We found there provisions and tools, which had been shipped by freight several weeks in advance. The building, erected in 1901 and enlarged in 1902, was found to have been blown by a storm from its foundation posts a few months previously. While we were awaiting the arrival of the shipment of machinery and parts from Dayton, we were busy putting the old building in repair, and erecting a new building to serve as a workshop for assembling and housing the new machine.

Just as the building was being completed, the parts and material for the machines arrived simultaneously with one of the worst storms that had visited Kitty Hawk in years. The storm came on suddenly, blowing 30 to 40 miles an hour.

It increased during the night, and the next day was blowing over 75 miles an hour. In order to save the tar-paper roof, we decided it would be necessary to get out in this wind and nail down more securely certain parts that were especially exposed. When I ascended the ladder and reached the edge of the roof, the wind caught under my large coat, blew it up around my head and bound my arms till I was perfectly helpless. Wilbur came to my assistance and held down my coat while I tried to drive the nails. But the wind was so strong I could not guide the hammer and succeeded in striking my fingers as often as the nails.

The next three weeks were spent in setting the motor-machine together. On days with more favorable winds we gained additional experience in handling a flyer by gliding with the 1902 machine, which we had found in pretty fair condition in the old building, where we had left it the year before.

Mr. Chanute and Dr. Spratt, who had been guests in our camp in 1901 and 1902, spent some time with us, but neither one was able to remain to see the test of the motor-machine, on account of the delays caused by trouble which developed in the propeller shafts.

While Mr. Chanute was with us, a good deal of time was spent in discussion of the mathematical calculations upon which we had based our machine. He informed us that, in designing machinery, about 20 per cent. was usually allowed for the loss in the transmission of power. As we had allowed only 5 per cent., a figure we had arrived at by some crude measurements of the friction of one of the chains when carrying only a very light load, we were much alarmed. More than the whole surplus in power allowed in our calculations would, according to Mr. Chanute's estimate, be consumed in friction in the driving chains. After Mr. Chanute's departure, we suspended one of the drive chains over a sprocket, hanging bags of sand on either side of the sprocket of a weight approximately equal to the pull that would be exerted on the chains when driving the propellers. By measuring the extra amount of weight needed on one side to lift the weight on the other, we calculated the loss in transmission. This indicated that the loss of power from this source would be only 5 per cent., as we originally estimated. But while we could see no serious error in this method of determining the loss, we were very uneasy until we had a chance to run the propellers with the motor to see whether we could get the estimated number of turns.

The first run of the motor on the machine developed a flaw in one of the propeller shafts which had not been discovered in the test at Dayton. The shafts were sent at once to Dayton for repair, and were not received again until November 20, having been gone two weeks. We immediately put them in the machine and made another test. A new trouble developed. The sprockets which were screwed on the shafts, and locked with nuts of opposite thread, persisted in coming loose. After many futile attempts to get them fast, we had to give it up for that day, and went to bed much discouraged. However, after a night's rest, we got up the next morning in better spirits and resolved to try again.

While in the bicycle business we had become well acquainted with the use of hard tire cement for fastening tires on the rims. We had once used it successfully in repairing a stop watch after several watchsmiths had told us it could not be repaired. If tire cement was good for fastening the hands on a stop watch, why should it not be good for fastening the sprockets on the propeller shaft of a flying machine? We decided to try it. We heated the shafts and sprockets, melted cement into the threads, and screwed them together again. This trouble was over. The sprockets stayed fast.

Just as the machine was ready for test bad weather set in. It had been disagreeably cold for several weeks, so cold that we could scarcely work on the machine for some days. But now we began to have rain and snow, and a wind of 25 to 30 miles blew for several days from the north. While we were being delayed by the weather we arranged a mechanism to measure automatically the duration of a flight from the time the machine started to move forward to the time it stopped, the distance traveled through the air in that time, and the number of revolutions made by the motor and propeller. A stop watch took the time; an anemometer measured the air traveled through; and a counter took the number of revolutions made by the propellers. The watch anemometer and revolution counter were all automatically started and stopped simultaneously. From data thus obtained we expected to prove or disprove the accuracy of our propeller calculations.

On November 28, while giving the motor a run indoors, we thought we again saw something wrong with one of the propeller shafts. On stopping the motor we discovered that one of the tubular shafts had cracked!

Immediate preparation was made for returning to Dayton to build another set of shafts. We decided to abandon the use of tubes, as they did not afford enough spring to take up the shocks of premature or missed explosions of the motor. Solid tool-steel shafts of smaller diameter than the tubes previously used were decided upon. These would allow a certain amount of spring. The tubular shafts were many times stronger than would have been necessary to transmit the power of our motor if the strains upon them had been uniform. But the large hollow shafts had no spring in them to absorb the unequal strains.

Wilbur remained in camp while I went to get the new shafts. I did not get back to camp again till Friday, the 11th of December. Saturday afternoon the machine was again ready for trial, but the wind was so light a start could not have been made from level ground with the run of only sixty feet permitted by our monorail track. Nor was there enough time before dark to take the machine to one of the hills, where, by placing the track on a steep incline, sufficient speed could be secured for starting in calm air.

Monday, December 14, was a beautiful day, but there was not enough wind to enable a start to be made from the level ground about camp. We therefore decided to attempt a flight from the side of the big Kill Devil Hill. We had arranged with the members of the Kill Devil Hill Life Saving Station, which was located a little over a mile from our camp, to inform them when we were ready to make the first trial of the machine. We were soon joined by J. T. Daniels, Robert Westcott, Thomas Beachem, W. S. Dough and Uncle Benny O'Neal, of the station, who helped us get the machine to the hill, a quarter mile away. We laid the track 150 feet up the side of the hill on a 9-degree slope. With the slope of the track, the thrust of the propellers and the machine starting directly into the wind, we did not anticipate any trouble in getting

up flying speed on the 60-foot monorail track. But we did not feel certain the operator could keep the machine balanced on the track.

When the machine had been fastened with a wire to the track, so that it could not start until released by the operator, and the motor had been run to make sure that it was in condition, we tossed up a coin to decide who should have the first trial. Wilbur won. I took a position at one of the wings, intending to help balance the machine as it ran down the track. But when the restraining wire was slipped, the machine started off so quickly I could stay with it only a few feet. After a 35 to 40-foot run it lifted from the rail. But it was allowed to turn up too much. It climbed a few feet, stalled, and then settled to the ground near the foot of the hill, 105 feet below. My stop watch showed that it had been in the air just 3½ seconds. In landing the left wing touched first. The machine swung around, dug the skids into the sand and broke one of them. Several other parts were also broken, but the damage to the machine was not serious. While the test had shown nothing as to whether the power of the motor was sufficient to keep the machine up, since the landing was made many feet below the starting point, the experiment had demonstrated that the method adopted for launching the machine was a safe and practical one. On the whole, we were much pleased.

Two days were consumed in making repairs, and the machine was not ready again till late in the afternoon of the 16th. While we had it out on the track in front of the building, making the final adjustments, a stranger came along. After looking at the machine a few seconds he inquired what it was. When we told him it was a flying machine he asked whether we intended to fly it. We said we did, as soon as we had a suitable wind. He looked at it several minutes longer and then, wishing to be courteous, remarked that it looked as if it would fly, if it had a "suitable wind." We were much amused, for, no doubt, he had in mind the recent 75-mile gale when he repeated our words, "a suitable wind!"

During the night of December 16, 1903, a strong cold wind blew from the north. When we arose on the morning of the 17th, the puddles of water, which had been standing about camp since the recent rains, were covered with ice. The wind had a velocity of 10 to 12 meters per second (22 to 27 miles an hour). We thought it would die down before long, and so remained indoors the early part of the morning. But when ten o'clock arrived, and the wind was as brisk as ever, we decided that we had better get the machine out and attempt a flight. We hung out the signal for the men of the life saving station. We thought that by facing the flyer into a strong wind, there ought to be no trouble in launching it from the level ground about camp. We realized the difficulties of flying in so high a wind, but estimated that the added dangers in flight would be partly compensated for by the slower speed in landing.

We laid the track on a smooth stretch of ground about one hundred feet north of the new building. The biting cold wind made work difficult, and we had to warm up frequently in our living room, where we had a good fire in an improvised stove made of a large carbide can. By the time all was ready, J. T. Daniels, W. S. Dough and A. D. Etheridge, members of the Kill Devil Life Saving Station; W. C. Brinkley, of Manteo, and Johnny Moore, a boy from Nag's Head, had arrived.

We had a "Richards" hand anemometer with which we measured the velocity of the wind.. Measurements made just before starting the first flight showed velocities of 11 to 12 meters per second, or 24 to 27 miles per hour. Measurements made just before the last flight gave between 9 and 10 meters per second. One made just after showed a little over 8 meters. The records of the Government Weather Bureau at Kitty Hawk gave the velocity of the wind between the hours of 10:30 and 12 o'clock, the time during which the four flights were made, as averaging 27 miles at the time of the first flight and 24 miles at the time of the last.

* * * * *

Wilbur, having used his turn in the unsuccessful attempt on the 14th, the right to the first trial now belonged to me. After running the motor a few minutes to heat it up, I released the wire that held the machine to the track, and the machine started forward into the wind. Wilbur ran at the side of the machine, holding the wing to balance it on the track. Unlike the start on the 14th, made in a calm, the machine, facing a 27-mile wind, started very slowly. Wilbur was able to stay with it till it lifted from the track after a forty-foot run. One of the life saving men snapped the camera for us, taking a picture just as the machine had reached the end of the track and had risen to a height of about two feet. The slow forward speed of the machine over the ground is clearly shown in the picture by Wilbur's attitude. He stayed along beside the machine without any effort.

The course of the flight up and down was exceedingly erratic, partly due to the irregularity of the air, and partly to lack of experience in handling this machine. The control of the front rudder was difficult on account of its being balanced too near the center. This gave it a tendency to turn itself when started; so that it turned too far on one side and then too far on the other. As a result the machine would rise suddenly to about ten feet, and then as suddenly dart for the ground. A sudden dart when a little over a hundred feet from the end of the track, or a little over 120 feet from the point at which it rose into the air, ended the flight. As the velocity of the wind was over 35 feet per second and the speed of the machine against this wind ten feet per second, the speed of the machine relative to the air was over 45 feet per second, and the length of the flight was equivalent to a flight of 540 feet made in calm air. This flight lasted only 12 seconds, but it was nevertheless the first in the history of the world in which a machine carrying a man had raised itself by its own power into the air in full flight, had sailed forward without reduction of speed, and had finally landed at a point as high as that from which it started.

* * * * *

At twenty minutes after eleven Wilbur tarted on the second flight. The course of this flight was much like that of the first, very much up and down. The speed over the ground was somewhat faster than that of the first flight, due to the lesser wind. The duration of the flight was less than a second longer than the first, but the distance covered was about seventy-five feet greater.

Twenty minutes later the third flight started. This one was steadier than the first one an hour before. I was proceeding along pretty well when a sudden gust from the right lifted the machine up twelve to fifteen feet and turned it up sidewise in an alarming manner. It began sliding off to the left. I warped the wings to try to recover the lateral balance and at the same time pointed the machine down to reach the ground as quickly as possible. The lateral control was more effective than I had imagined and before I reached the ground the right wing was lower than the left and struck first. The time of this flight was fifteen seconds and the distance over the ground a little over 200 feet.

Wilbur started the fourth and last flight at just 12 o'clock. The first few hundred feet were up and down as before, but by the time three hundred feet had been covered, the machine was under much better control. The course for the next four or five hundred feet had but little undulation. However, when out about eight hundred feet the machine began pitching again, and, in one of its starts downward, struck the ground. The distance over the ground was measured and found to be 852 feet; the time of the flight 59 seconds. The frame supporting the front rudder was badly broken, but the main part of the machine was not injured at all. We estimated that the machine could be put in condition for flight again in a day or two.

While we were standing about discussing this last flight, a sudden strong gust of wind struck the machine and began to turn it over. Everybody made a rush for it. Wilbur, who was at one end, seized it in front, Mr. Daniels and I, who were behind, tried to stop it behind, tried to stop it by holding to the rear uprights. All our efforts were vain. The machine rolled over and over. Daniels, who had retained his grip, was carried along with it, and was thrown about head over heels inside of the machine. Fortunately he was not seriously injured, though badly bruised in falling about against the motor, chain guides, etc. The ribs in the surfaces of the machine were broken, the motor injured and the chain guides badly bent, so that all possibility of further flights with it for that year were at an end.

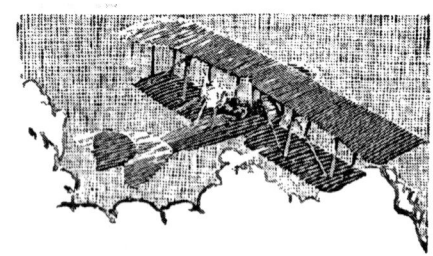

Some Aeronautical Experiments

By Wilbur Wright

THE difficulties which obstruct the pathway to success in flying machine construction are of three general classes: (1) Those which relate to the construction of the sustaining wings. (2) Those which relate to the generation and application of the power required to drive the machine through the air. (3) Those relating to the balancing and steering of the machine after it is actually in flight. Of these difficulties two are already to a certain extent solved. Men already know how to construct wings or aeroplanes which, when driven through air at sufficient speed, will not only sustain the weight of the wings themselves, but also that of the engine, and of the engineer as well. Men also know how to build engines and screws of sufficient lightness and power to drive these planes at sustaining speed. As long ago as 1893 a machine weighing 8,000 lbs. demonstrated its power both to lift itself from the ground and to maintain a speed of from 30 to 40 miles per hour; but it came to grief in an accidental free flight, owing to the inability of the operators to balance and steer it properly. This inability to balance and steer still confronts students of the flying problem, although nearly ten years have passed. When this one feature has been worked out the age of flying machines will have arrived, for all other difficulties are of minor importance.

The person who merely watches the flight of a bird gathers the impression that the bird has nothing to think of but the flapping of its wings. As a matter of fact, this is a very small part of its mental labour. Even to mention all the things the bird must constantly keep in mind in order to fly securely through the air would take a very considerable treatise. If I take a piece of paper, and after placing it parallel with the ground, quickly let it fall, it will not settle steadily down as a staid, sensible piece of paper ought to do, but it insists on contravening every recognized rule of decorum, turning over and darting hither and thither in the most erratic manner, much after the style of an untrained horse. Yet this is the style of steed that men must learn to manage before flying can become an everyday sport. The bird has learned this art of equilibrium, and learned it so thoroughly that its skill is not apparent to our sight. We only learn to appreciate it when we try to imitate it. Now, there are two ways of learning how to ride a fractious horse: one is to get on him and learn by actual practice how each motion and trick may be best met; the other is to sit on a fence and watch the beast awhile, and then retire to the house and at leisure figure out the best way of overcoming his jumps and kicks. The latter system is the safest; but the former, on the whole, turns out the larger porportion of good riders. It is very much the same in learning to ride a flying machine; if you are looking for perfect safety you will do well to sit on a fence and watch the birds; but if you really wish to learn you must mount a machine and become acquainted with its tricks by actual trial.

* * * * * *

My own active interest in aeronautical problems dates back to the death of Lilienthal in 1896. The brief notice of his death which appeared in the telegraphic news at that time aroused a passive interest which had existed from my childhood, and led me to take down from the shelves of our home library a book on "Animal Mechanism," by Prof. Marey, which I had already read several times. From this I was led to read more modern works, and as my brother soon became equally interested with myself, we soon passed from the reading to the thinking, and finally to the working stage. It seemed to us that the main reason why the problem had remained so long unsolved was that no one had been able to obtain any adequate practice. We figured that Lilienthal in five years of time had spent only about five hours in actual gliding through the air. The wonder was not that he had done so little, but that he had accomplished so much. It would not be considered at all safe for a bicycle rider to attempt to ride through a crowded city street after only five hours' practice, spread out in bits of ten seconds each over a period of five years; yet Lilienthal with this brief practice was remarkably successful in meeting the fluctuations and eddies of wind gusts. We thought that if some method could be found by which it would be possible to practice by the hour instead of by the second there would be hope of advancing the solution of a very difficult problem. It seemed feasible to do this by building a machine which would be sustained at a speed of 18 miles per hour, and then finding a locality where winds of this velocity were common. With these conditions a rope attached to the machine to keep it from floating backward would answer very nearly the same purpose as a propeller driven by a motor, and it would be possible to practice by the hour, and without any serious danger, as it would not be necessary to rise far from the ground, and the machine would not have any forward motion at all. We found, according to the accepted tables of air pressures on curved surfaces, that a machine spreading 200 square feet of wing surface would be sufficient for our purpose, and that places could easily be found along the Atlantic coast where winds of 16 to 25 miles were not at all uncommon. When the winds were low it was our plan to glide from the tops of sand hills, and when they were sufficiently strong to use a rope for our motor and fly over one spot. Our next work was to draw up the plan for a suitable machine. After much study we finally concluded that tails were a source of trouble rather than of assistance, and therefore we decided to dispense with them altogether. It seemed reasonable that if the body of the operator could be placed in a horizontal position instead of the upright, as in the machines of Lilienthal, Pilcher and Chanute, the wind resistance could be very materially reduced, since only one square foot instead of five would be exposed. As a full half-horse-power could be saved by this change, we arranged to try at least the horizontal position. Then the method of control used by Lilienthal, which consisted in shifting the body, did not seem quite as quick or effective as the case required; so, after long study, we contrived a system consisting of two large surfaces on the Chanute double-deck plan, and a smaller surface placed a short distance in front of the main surfaces in such a position that the action of the wind upon it would counterbalance the effect of the travel of the center of pressure on the main surfaces. Thus changes in the direction and velocity of the wind would have little disturbing effect, and the operator would be required to attend only to the steering of the machine, which was to be effected by curving the forward surface up or down. The lateral equilibrium and the steering to right or left was to be attained by a peculiar torsion of the main surfaces, which was equivalent to presenting one end of the wings at a greater angle than the other. In the main frame a few changes were also made in the details of construction and trussing employed by Mr. Chanute. The most important of these were: (1) The moving of the forward main cross-piece of the frame to the extreme front edge; (2) the encasing in the cloth of all cross-pieces and ribs of the surfaces; (3) a rearrangement of the wires used in trussing the two surfaces together, which rendered it possible to tighten all the wires by simply shortening two of them.

With these plans we proceeded in the summer of 1900 to Kitty Hawk, North Carolina, a little settlement located on the strip of land that separates Albemarle Sound from the Atlantic Ocean. Owing to the impossibility of obtaining suitable material for a 200-square-foot machine, we were compelled to make it only 165 square feet in area, which, according to the Lilienthal tables, would be supported at an angle of three degrees in a wind of about 21 miles per hour. On the very day that the machine was completed the wind blew from 25 to 30 miles per hour, and we took it out for a trial as a kite. We found that while it was supported with a man on it in a wind of about 25 miles, its angle was much nearer 20 degrees than three degrees. Even in gusts of 30 miles the angle of incidence did not get as low as three degrees, although the wind at this speed has more than twice the lifting power of a 21-mile wind. As winds of 30 miles per hour are not plen-

tiful on clear days, it was at once evident that our plan of practicing by the hour, day after day, would have to be postponed. Our system of twisting the surfaces to regulate the lateral balance was tried and found to be much more effective than shifting the operator's body. On subsequent days, when the wind was too light to support the machine with a man on it, we tested it as a kite, working the rudders by cords reaching to the ground. The results were very satisfactory, yet we were well aware that this method of testing is never wholly convincing until the results are confirmed by actual gliding experience.

We then turned our attention to making a series of actual measurements of the lift and drift of the machine under various loads. So far as we were aware, this had never previously been done with any full-size machine. The results obtained were most astonishing, for it appeared that the total horizontal pull of the machine, while sustaining a weight of 52 lbs., was only 8.5 lbs., which was less than had previously been estimated for head resistance of the framing alone. Making allowance for the weight carried, it appeared that the head resistance of the framing was but little more than 50 per cent. of the amount which Mr. Chanute had estimated as the head resistance of the framing of his machine. On the other hand, it appeared sadly deficient in lifting power as compared with the calculated lift of curved surfaces of its size. This deficiency we supposed might be due to one or more of the following causes:—(1) That the depth of the curvature of our surfaces was insufficient, being only about one in 22, instead of one in 12. (2) That the cloth used in our wings was not sufficiently airtight. (3) That the Lilienthal tables might themselves be somewhat in error. We decided to arrange our machine for the following year so that the depth of the curvature of its surfaces could be varied at will and its covering airproofed.

Our attention was next turned to gliding, but no hill suitable for the purpose could be found near our camp at Kitty Hawk. This compelled us to take the machine to a point four miles south, where the Kill Devil sand hill rises from the flat sand to a height of more than 100 feet. Its main slope is toward the northeast, and has an inclination of 10 degrees. On the day of our arrival the wind blew about 25 miles an hour, and as we had had no experience at all in gliding, we deemed it unsafe to attempt to leave the ground. But on the day following, the wind having subsided to 14 miles per hour, we made about a dozen glides. It had been the original intention that the operator should run with the machine to obtain initial velocity, and assume the horizontal position only after the machine was in free flight. When it came time to land he was to resume the upright position and alight on his feet, after the style of previous gliding experiments. But in actual trial we found it much better to employ the help of two assistants in starting, which the peculiar form of our machine enabled us readily to do; and in landing we found that it was entirely practicable to land while still reclining in a horizontal position upon the machine. Although the landings were made while moving at speeds of more than 20 miles an hour, neither machine nor operator suffered any injury. The slope of the hill was 9.5 deg., or a drop of one foot in six. We found that after attaining a speed of about 25 to 30 miles with reference to the wind, or 10 to 15 miles over the ground, the machine not only glided parallel to the slope of the hill, but greatly increased its speed, thus indicating its ability to glide on a somewhat less angle than 9.5 deg., when we should feel it safe to rise higher from the surface. The control of the machine proved even better than we had dared to expect, responding quickly to the slightest motion of the rudder. With these glides our experiments for the year 1900 closed. Although the hours and hours of practice we had hoped to obtain finally dwindled down to about two minutes, we were very much pleased with the general results of the trip, for, setting out as we did with almost revolutionary theories on many points and an entirely untried form of machine, we considered it quite a point to be able to return without having our pet theories completely knocked on the head by the hard logic of experience, and our own brains dashed out in the bargain. Everything seemed to us to confirm the correctness of our original opinions—(1) that practice is the key to the secret of flying; (2) that it is practicable to assume the horizontal position; (3) that a smaller surface set at a negative angle in front of the main bearing surfaces, or wings, will largely counteract the effect of the fore and aft travel of the center of pressure; (4) that steering up and down can be attained with a rudder without moving the position of the operator's body; (5) that twisting the wings so as to present their ends to the wind at different angles is a more prompt and efficient way of maintaining lateral equilibrium than that employed in shifting the body of the operator of the machine.

When the time came to design our new machine for 1901 we decided to make it exactly like the previous machine in theory and method of operation. But as the former machine was not able to support the weight of the operator when flown as a kite, except in very high winds and at very large angles of incidence, we decided to increase its lifting power. Accordingly, the curvature of the surfaces was increased to one in 12, to conform to the shape on which Lilienthal's table was based, and to be on the safe side we decided also to increase the area of the machine from 165 square feet to 308 square feet, although so large a machine had never before been deemed controllable. The Lilienthal machine had an area of 151 square feet; that of Pilcher, 165 square feet; and the Chanute doubledecker, 134 square feet. As our system of control consisted in a manipulation of the surfaces themselves instead of shifting the operator's body, we hoped that the new machine would be controllable, notwithstanding its great size. According to calculations, it would obtain support in a wind of 17 miles per hour with an angle of incidence of only three degrees.

Our experience of the previous year having shown the necessity of a suitable building for housing the machine, we erected a cheap frame building, 16 feet wide, 25 feet long, and 7 feet high at the eaves. As our machine was 22 feet wide, 14 feet long (including the rudder), and about 6 feet high, it was not necessary to take the machine apart in any way in order to house it. Both ends of the building, except the gable parts, were made into doors which hinged above, so that when opened they formed an awning at each end and left an entrance the full width of the building. We went into camp about the middle of July, and were soon joined by Mr. E. C. Huffaker, of Tennessee, an experienced aeronautical investigator in the employ of Mr. Chanute, by whom his services were kindly loaned, and by Dr. A. G. Spratt, of Pennsylvania, a young man who has made some valuable investigations of the properties of variously curved surfaces and the travel of the center of pressure thereon. Early in August Mr. Chanute came down from Chicago to witness our experiments, and spent a week in camp with us. These gentlemen, with my brother and myself, formed our camping party, but in addition we had in many of our experiments the valuable assistance of Mr. W. J. Tate and Mr. Dan Tate, of Kitty Hawk.

* * * * * *

It had been our intention when building the machine to do most of the experimenting in the following manner: —When the wind blew 17 miles an hour, or more, we would attach a rope to the machine and let it rise as a kite with the operator upon it. When it should reach a proper height the operator would cast off the rope and glide down to the ground just as from the top of a hill. In this way we would be saved the trouble of carrying the machine uphill after each glide, and could make at least 10 glides in the time required for one in the other way. But when we came to try it we found that a wind of 17 miles, as measured by Richards' anemometer, instead of sustaining the machine with its operator, a total weight of 240 lbs., at an angle of incidence of three degrees, in reality would not sustain the machine alone—100 lbs. —at this angle. Its lifting capacity seemed scarcely one-third of the calculated amount. In order to make sure that this was not due to the porosity of the cloth, we constructed two small experimental surfaces of equal size, one of which was air-proofed and the other left in its natural state; but we could detect no difference in their lifting powers.

For a time we were led to suspect that the lift of curved surfaces little exceeded that of planes of the same size, but further investigation and experiment led to the opinion that (1) the anemometer used by us over-recorded the true velocity of the wind by nearly 15 per cent.; (2) that the well-known Smeaton coefficient of $.005 V^2$ for the wind pressure at 90 degrees is probably too great by at least 20 per cent.; (3) that Lilienthal's estimate that the pressure on a curved surface having an angle of incidence of three degrees equals .545 of the pressure at 90 degrees is too large, being nearly 50 per cent. greater than very recent experiments of our own with a special pressure testing machine indicate; (4) that the superposition of the surfaces somewhat reduced the lift per square foot, as compared with a single surface of equal area.

In gliding experiments, however, the amount of lift is of less relative importance than the ratio of lift to drift, as this alone decides the angle of gliding descent. In a plane the pressure is always perpendicular to the surface, and the ratio of lift to drift is therefore the same as that of the cosine to the sine of the angle of incidence. But in curved surfaces a very remarkable situation is found. The pressure, instead of being uniformly normal to the chord of the arc, is usually inclined considerably in front of the perpendicular. The result is that the lift is greater and the drift less than if the pressure were normal. Lilienthal was the first to discover this exceedingly though our measurements differ considerably from those of Lilienthal. While important fact, which is fully set forth in his book, "Bird Flight the Basis of the Flying Art," but owing to some errors in the methods he used in making measurements, question was raised by other investigators not only as to the accuracy of his figures, but even as to the existence of any tangential force at all. Our experiments confirm the existence of this force, at Kitty Hawk we spent much time in measuring the horizontal pressure on our unloaded machine at various angles of incidence. We found that at 13 degrees the horizontal pressure was about 23 lbs. This included not only the drift proper, or horizontal component of the pressure on the side of the surface, but also the head resistance of the framing as well. The weight of the machine at the time of this test was about 108 lbs. Now, if the pressure had been normal to the chord of the surface, the drift proper would have been to the lift (108 lbs.) as the sine of 13 degrees is to the cosine of 13 degrees, or $\frac{.22 \times 108}{.97} = 24 +$ lbs.; but this slightly exceeds the total pull of 23 lbs. on our scales. Therefore, it is evident that the average pressure on the surface, instead of being normal to the chord, was so far inclined toward the front that all the head resistance of framing and wires used in the construction was more than overcome. In a wind of 14 miles per hour resistance is by no means a negligible factor, so that tangential is evidently a force of considerable value. In a higher wind, which sustained the machine at an angle of 10 degrees, the pull on the scales was 18 lbs. With the pressure normal to the chord the drift proper would have been $\frac{.17 \times 98}{.98} = 17$ lbs., so that, although the higher wind velocity must have caused an increase in

the head resistance, the tangential force still came within one pound of overcoming it. After our return from Kitty Hawk we began a series of experiments to accurately determine the amount and direction of the pressure produced on curved surfaces when acted upon by winds at the various angles from zero to 90 degrees. These experiments are not yet concluded, but in general they support Lilienthal in the claim that the curves give pressures more favorable in amount and direction than planes; but we find marked differences in the exact values, especially at angles below 10 degrees. We were unable to obtain direct measurements of the horizontal pressures of the machine with the operator on board, but by comparing the distance traveled in gliding with the vertical fall, it was easily calculated that at a speed of 24 miles per hour the total horizontal resistance of our machine when bearing the operator, amounted to 40 lbs., which is equivalent to about 2 1/3 horse-power. It must not be supposed, however, that a motor developing this power would be sufficient to drive a man-bearing machine. The extra weight of the motor would require either a larger machine, higher speed, or a greater angle of incidence in order to support it, and therefore more power. It is probable, however, that an engine of six horse-power, weighing 100 lbs., would answer the purpose. Such an engine is entirely practicable. Indeed, working motors of one-half this weight per horse-power (9 lbs. per horse-power) have been constructed by several different builders. Increasing the speed of our machine from 24 to 33 miles per hour reduced the total horizontal pressure from 40 to about 35 lbs. This was quite an advantage in gliding, as it made it possible to sail about 15 per cent. further with a given drop. However, it would be of little or no advantage in reducing the size of the motor in a power-driven machine, because the lessened thrust would be counter-balanced by the increased speed per minute. Some years ago Professor Langley called attention to the great economy of thrust which might be obtained by using very high speeds, and from this many were led to suppose that high speed was essential to success in a motor-driven machine. But the economy to which Professor Langley called attention was in foot-pounds per mile of travel, not in foot pounds per minute. It is the foot-pounds per minute that fixes the size of the motor. The probability is that the first flying machines will have a relatively low speed, perhaps not much exceeding 20 miles per hour, but the problem of increasing the speed will be much simpler in some respects than that of increasing the speed of a steamboat; for, whereas in the latter case the size of the engine must increase as the cube of the speed, in the flying machine, until extremely high speeds are reached, the capacity of the motor increases in less than simple ratio; and there is even a decrease in the fuel consumption per mile of travel. In other words, to double the speed of a steamship (and the same is true of the balloon type of airship) eight times the engine and boiler capacity would be required, and four times the fuel consumption per mile of travel; while a flying machine would require engines of less than double the size, and there would be an actual decrease in the fuel consumption per mile of travel. But looking at the matter conversely, the great disadvantage of the flying machine is apparent;

for in the latter no flight at all is possible unless the proportion of horse-power to flying capacity is very high; but on the other hand a steamship is a mechanical success if its ratio of horse-power to tonnage is insignificant. A flying machine that would fly at a speed of 50 miles an hour with engines of 1,000 horse-power would not be upheld by its wings at all at a speed of less than 25 miles an hour, and nothing less than 500 horse-power could drive it at this speed. But a boat which could make 40 miles per hour with engines of 1,000 horse-power would still move four miles an hour even if the engines were reduced to one horse-power. The problems of land and water travel were solved in the nineteenth century, because it was possible to begin with small achievements and gradually work up to our present success. The flying prolem was left over to the twentieth century, because in this case the art must be highly developed before any flight of any considerable duration at all can be obtained.

However, there is another way of flying which requires no artificial motor, and many workers believe that success will first come by this road. I refer to the soaring flight, by which the machine is permanently sustained in the air by the same means that are employed by soaring birds. They spread their wings to the wind, and sail by the hour, with no perceptible exertion beyond that required to balance and steer themselves. What sustains them is not definitely known, though it is almost certain that it is a rising current of air. But whether it be a rising current or something else, it is as well able to support a flying machine as a bird, if man once learns the art of utilizing it. In gliding experiments it has long been known that the rate of vertical descent is very much retarded, and the duration of the flight greatly prolonged, if a strong wind blows up the face of the hill parallel to its surface. Our machine, when gliding in still air, has a rate of vertical descent of nearly six feet per second, while in a wind blowing 26 miles per hour up a steep hill we made glides in which the rate of descent was less than two feet per second. And during the larger part of this time, while the machine remained exactly in the rising current, there was no descent at all, but even a slight rise. If the operator had had sufficient skill to keep himself from passing beyond the rising current he would have been sustained indefinitely at a higher point than that from which he started.

* * * * * *

In looking over our experiments of the past two years, with models and full-size machines, the following points stand out with clearness:—

1. That the lifting power of a large machine, held stationary in a wind at a small distance from the earth, is much less than the Lilienthal table and our own laboratory experiments would lead us to expect. When the machine is moved through the air, as in gliding, the discrepancy seems much less marked.

2. That the ratio of drift to lift in well-balanced surfaces is less at angles of incidence of five degrees to 12 degrees than at an angle of three degrees.

3. That in arched surfaces the center of pressure at 90 degrees is near the center of the surface, but moves slowly for-

ward as the angle becomes less, till a critical angle varying with the shape and depth of the curve is reached, after which it moves rapidly toward the rear till the angle of no lift is found.

4. That with similar conditions large surfaces may be controlled with not much greater difficulty than small ones, if the control is effected by manipulation of the surfaces themselves, rather than by a movement of the body of the operator.

5. That the head resistances of the framing can be brought to a point much below that usually estimated as necessary.

6. That tails, both vertical and horizontal, may with safety be eliminated in gliding and other flying experiments.

7. That a horizontal position of the operator's body may be assumed without excessive danger, and thus the head resistance reduced to about one-fifth that of the upright position.

8. That a pair of superposed, or tandem, surfaces has less lift in proportion to drift than either surface separately, even after making allowance for weight and head resistance of the connections.

THIS BOOK IS DUE ON THE LAST DATE
STAMPED BELOW

EARHOTA98